Sibling Petitioning Brother or Sister

Petitioning your Brother or Sister if you are a U.S. Citizen to become a Lawful Permanent Resident

Attorney Brian D. Lerner

BDL LAW OFFICES OF BRIAN D. LERNER A PROFESSIONAL CORPORATION

ATTORNEY DRAFTED IMMIGRATION PETITIONS

By

Brian D. Lerner

Attorney at Law

Disclaimer and Terms of Use:

Effort has been made to ensure that the information in this book is accurate and complete. However, the author and the publisher do not warrant that this particular petition will mirror or be exactly as your situation. There has not been any attorney-client agreement created by the purchase of this petition or application. No legal advice has occurred. The cases, regulations and/or statutes cited may change at any time without notice.

ISBN: 978-1-958990-40-7

INTRODUCTION

There are a multitude of different immigration petitions and applications. They are complex and full of requirements. Obviously, it would be best to hire an immigration attorney to best prepare the petitions and applications. However, this can certainly cost thousands of dollars.

The next best option is to get a sample of the petition written by an experienced immigration attorney. The samples cost a fraction what would be charged by an immigration attorney. However, while the reader has to alter, amend and change the parts of the sample petition to reflect their actual situation, it is a fantastic roadmap for them to use. If the reader has purchased the entire petition or application, they will have real live samples of cover letters, forms, declarations, affidavits and the necessary exhibits to use. The samples come from real cases and the names of those clients have been redacted to protect the privacy of that person or corporation.

These are petitions and applications that have been drafted by an experienced immigration attorney with over 25 years of experience. Get the benefits of that experience without the costs.

CONTENTS

About the Law Offices of Brian D. Lerner

The Law Offices of Brian D. Lerner, APC. The law practice consists of Immigration and Nationality Law and everything involved with and regarding immigration which includes citizenship, investment visas, family and employment visas, removal and deportation hearings, appeals, waivers, adjustment, consulate processing and all types of immigration and citizenship matters. Thousands of families have been reunited and/or permitted to stay in the U.S. and/or return to the U.S. because of the successful work of Immigration Attorney Brian D. Lerner.

This law offices handles all types of immigration cases including family based and employment based. Immigration issues range from immigration court proceedings to trying to fix what paralegals may have done that was neither correct nor proper. Foreign nationals must have experience lawyers admitted to practice law.

The Law Offices of Brian D. Lerner, APC, handles cases arising from business visas, work permits, Green Cards, non-immigrant visas, deportation, citizenship, appeals and all areas of immigration. The Law Offices of Brian D. Lerner, APC does EB-5 Investor Visas, H-1B Specialty Occupation, L-1 Intracompany Transferee, E-2 Treaty Investor, E-1 Treaty Trader, O-1 Extraordinary Ability among others. Regarding immigrant visas for the Green Card, the firm does PERM and advanced degree PERM, Family Petitions, and Extraordinary Alien Petitions. In addition to affirmative petitions, the Law Firm represents people in people in deportation and removal hearings, including political asylum, withholding of removal, and convention against torture cases.

Brian D. Lerner has been certified as an expert in Immigration & Nationality Law by the California State Bar, Board of Legal Specialization since 2000 and has been re-certified three times. He now passes on his decades of experience by allowing the Reader, Law Schools, Professors and other Immigration Attorneys to purchase sample petitions on every facet of Immigration Law.

About the Sibling I-130 Petition

Ready to Petition your Brother or Sister? In this case, are you a United States Citizen over 21 years old petitioning a sibling? It will be considered a fourth preference petition where there will be visa waiting for quite a while before you can move onto the next phase. The next step when the visa number becomes current is to either adjust status or consulate process. The first part must be done and must be done properly in order to ever proceed to the next part. Without a proper I-130 application there will never be a Green Card. If approved, then you could move onto the next step in the immigration process. If not approved, it will take years of red tape. Remember, it is your responsibility to submit everything correctly. This sample I-130 Petition has everything necessary to give you the best chance possible to get an approval. Just input your own information and use the application as a guide. It has been prepared by an expert immigration attorney. Thus, this book will allow you to see a guide of how it is done, prepared and submitted.

ATTORNEY COVER LETTER

Law Offices of Brian D. Lerner

A PROFESSIONAL CORPORATION

CERTIFIED SPECIALIST IN IMMIGRATION AND NATIONALITY LAW
ADMITTED TO THE U.S. SUPREME COURT

LONG BEACH, CALIFORNIA
(562) 495-0554

May 2, 2019

U.S. Citizenship and Immigration Services
Attn: I-130
PO Box 21700
Phoenix, AZ 85036

Re: I-130, Petition for Alien Relative
Petitioner:
Beneficiary:

Dear Sir/Madam:

We hereby submit an I-130, Petition for Alien Relative, for (hereinafter "Petitioner") on behalf of his sister, (herein "Beneficiary").

Enclosed herein please find the following documents:

FORMS

Forms:	Description:
G-1145	E-Notification of Application/Petition Acceptance;
G-28	Notice of Entry of Appearance as Attorney or Accredited Representative (Petitioner);
G-28	Notice of Entry of Appearance as Attorney or Accredited Representative (Beneficiary); and
I-130	Petition for Alien Relative with $535.00 filing fee.

EXHIBITS

Exhibit:	Description:
'1'	United States Passport (or Naturalization Certificate) and Birth Certificate of the Petitioner with an English Translation;
'2'	California State Driver's License and Birth Certificate of the Beneficiary with an English Translation;
'3'	Photographs of the Petitioner and Beneficiary showing Sibling Relationship; and
'4'	Marriage Certificate of the Petitioner and Benificiary's Mother and Father .

Under the Immigration and Nationality Act ("INA") 201 (b)(2)(A)(i), the Immediate Relatives, including children, spouses and parents, and brothers/sisters of U.S. citizens may be petitioned for immigrant visas, without being subjected to direct numerical limitations.

In the present case the Petitioner is a naturalized U.S. citizen and the Beneficiary is his Sister. ***See* Exhibit 1**. Therefore, the Petitioner is qualified to file an Alien Relative Petition on behalf of his Sister, the Beneficiary. Based on the foregoing, we respectfully submit that the attached evidence shows the necessary relationship exists and that the instant I-130 should be approved. ***See* Exhibits 1-4.**

Thank you for your consideration in this matter. Should you have any further questions, please feel free to contact our office at (562) 495-0554.

Sincerely,

Attorney at Law

FORMS

e-Notification of Application/Petition Acceptance

Department of Homeland Security
U.S. Citizenship and Immigration Services

USCIS
Form G-1145

What Is the Purpose of This Form?

Use this form to request an electronic notification (e-Notification) when U.S. Citizenship and Immigration Services accepts your immigration application. This service is available for applications filed at a USCIS Lockbox facility.

General Information

Complete the information below and clip this form to the first page of your application package. You will receive one e-mail and/or text message for each form you are filing.

We will send the e-Notification within 24 hours after we accept your application. Domestic customers will receive an e-mail and/or text message; overseas customers will only receive an e-mail. Undeliverable e-Notifications cannot be resent.

The e-mail or text message will display your receipt number and tell you how to get updated case status information. It will not include any personal information. The e-Notification does not grant any type of status or benefit; rather it is provided as a convenience to customers.

USCIS will also mail you a receipt notice (I-797C), which you will receive within 10 days after your application has been accepted; use this notice as proof of your pending application or petition.

USCIS Privacy Act Statement

AUTHORITIES: The information requested on this form is collected pursuant to section 103(a) of the Immigration and Nationality Act, as amended INA section 101, et seq.

PURPOSE: The primary purpose for providing the information on this form is to request an electronic notification when USCIS accepts immigration form. The information you provide will be used to send you a text and/or email message.

DISCLOSURE: The information you provide is voluntary. However, failure to provide the requested information may prevent USCIS from providing you a text and/or email message receipting your immigration form.

ROUTINE USES: The information provided on this form will be used by and disclosed to DHS personnel and contractors in accordance with approved routine uses, as described in the associated published system of records notices [DHS/USCIS-007 - Benefits Information System and DHS/USCIS-001 - Alien File (A-File) and Central Index System (CIS), which can be found at www.dhs.gov/privacy]. The information may also be made available, as appropriate for law enforcement purposes or in the interest of national security.

Complete this form and clip it on top of the first page of your immigration form(s).

Applicant/Petitioner Full Last Name	Applicant/Petitioner Full First Name	Applicant/Petitioner Full Middle Name
[redacted]	[redacted]	[redacted]

Email Address	Mobile Phone Number (Text Message)
[redacted]	[redacted]

Notice of Entry of Appearance as Attorney or Accredited Representative

Department of Homeland Security

DHS Form G-28
OMB No. 1615-0105
Expires 05/31/2021

Part 1. Information About Attorney or Accredited Representative

1. USCIS Online Account Number (if any) ►

Name of Attorney or Accredited Representative

2.a. Family Name (Last Name): Lerner
2.b. Given Name (First Name): Brian
2.c. Middle Name: David

Address of Attorney or Accredited Representative

3.a. Street Number and Name: 3233 E Broadway
3.b. ☐ Apt. ☐ Ste. ☐ Flr.
3.c. City or Town: Long Beach
3.d. State: CA 3.e. ZIP Code: 90803
3.f. Province
3.g. Postal Code
3.h. Country: USA

Contact Information of Attorney or Accredited Representative

4. Daytime Telephone Number: 5624950554
5. Mobile Telephone Number (if any)
6. Email Address (if any): blerner@californiaimmigration.us
7. Fax Number (if any): 5626088672

Part 2. Eligibility Information for Attorney or Accredited Representative

Select **all applicable** items.

1.a. ☒ I am an attorney eligible to practice law in, and a member in good standing of, the bar of the highest courts of the following states, possessions, territories, commonwealths, or the District of Columbia. If you need extra space to complete this section, use the space provided in **Part 6. Additional Information**.

Licensing Authority: Supreme Court of California

1.b. Bar Number (if applicable): 158536

1.c. I (select **only one** box) ☐ am not ☐ am subject to any order suspending, enjoining, restraining, disbarring, or otherwise restricting me in the practice of law. If you are subject to any orders, use the space provided in **Part 6. Additional Information** to provide an explanation.

1.d. Name of Law Firm or Organization (if applicable): Law Offices of Brian D. Lerner, APC

2.a. ☐ I am an accredited representative of the following qualified nonprofit religious, charitable, social service, or similar organization established in the United States and recognized by the Department of Justice in accordance with 8 CFR part 1292.

2.b. Name of Recognized Organization

2.c. Date of Accreditation (mm/dd/yyyy)

3. ☐ I am associated with ________, the attorney or accredited representative of record who previously filed Form G-28 in this case, and my appearance as an attorney or accredited representative for a limited purpose is at his or her request.

4.a. ☐ I am a law student or law graduate working under the direct supervision of the attorney or accredited representative of record on this form in accordance with the requirements in 8 CFR 292.1(a)(2).

4.b. Name of Law Student or Law Graduate

Part 3. Notice of Appearance as Attorney or Accredited Representative

If you need extra space to complete this section, use the space provided in **Part 6. Additional Information**.

This appearance relates to immigration matters before (select **only one** box):

1.a. [X] U.S. Citizenship and Immigration Services (USCIS)

1.b. List the form numbers or specific matter in which appearance is entered.

I-130

2.a. [ ] U.S. Immigration and Customs Enforcement (ICE)

2.b. List the specific matter in which appearance is entered.

3.a. [ ] U.S. Customs and Border Protection (CBP)

3.b. List the specific matter in which appearance is entered.

4. Receipt Number (if any)

►

5. I enter my appearance as an attorney or accredited representative at the request of the (select **only one** box):

[ ] Applicant [ ] Petitioner [ ] Requestor
[ ] Beneficiary/Derivative [ ] Respondent (ICE, CBP)

Information About Client (Applicant, Petitioner, Requestor, Beneficiary or Derivative, Respondent, or Authorized Signatory for an Entity)

6.a. Family Name (Last Name)

6.b. Given Name (First Name)

6.c. Middle Name

7.a. Name of Entity (if applicable)

7.b. Title of Authorized Signatory for Entity (if applicable)

8. Client's USCIS Online Account Number (if any)

►

9. Client's Alien Registration Number (A-Number) (if any)

► A-

Client's Contact Information

10. Daytime Telephone Number

11. Mobile Telephone Number (if any)

12. Email Address (if any)

Mailing Address of Client

NOTE: Provide the client's mailing address. **Do not** provide the business mailing address of the attorney or accredited representative **unless** it serves as the safe mailing address on the application or petition being filed with this Form G-28.

13.a. Street Number and Name

13.b. [ ] Apt. [ ] Ste. [ ] Flr.

13.c. City or Town

13.d. State CA **13.e.** ZIP Code 60435

13.f. Province

13.g. Postal Code

13.h. Country

USA

Part 4. Client's Consent to Representation and Signature

Consent to Representation and Release of Information

I have requested the representation of and consented to being represented by the attorney or accredited representative named in **Part 1.** of this form. According to the Privacy Act of 1974 and U.S. Department of Homeland Security (DHS) policy, I also consent to the disclosure to the named attorney or accredited representative of any records pertaining to me that appear in any system of records of USCIS, ICE, or CBP.

Part 4. Client's Consent to Representation and Signature (continued)

Options Regarding Receipt of USCIS Notices and Documents

USCIS will send notices to both a represented party (the client) and his, her, or its attorney or accredited representative either through mail or electronic delivery. USCIS will send all secure identity documents and Travel Documents to the client's U.S. mailing address.

If you want to have notices and/or secure identity documents sent to your attorney or accredited representative of record rather than to you, please select **all applicable** items below. You may change these elections through written notice to USCIS.

1.a. [X] I request that USCIS send original notices on an application or petition to the U.S. business address of my attorney or accredited representative as listed in this form.

1.b. [ ] I request that USCIS send any secure identity document (Permanent Resident Card, Employment Authorization Document, or Travel Document) that I receive to the U.S. business address of my attorney or accredited representative (or to a designated military or diplomatic address in a foreign country (if permitted)).

NOTE: If your notice contains Form I-94, Arrival-Departure Record, USCIS will send the notice to the U.S. business address of your attorney or accredited representative. If you would rather have your Form I-94 sent directly to you, select **Item Number 1.c.**

1.c. [X] I request that USCIS send my notice containing Form I-94 to me at my U.S. mailing address.

Signature of Client or Authorized Signatory for an Entity

2.a. Signature of Client or Authorized Signatory for an Entity

➡

2.b. Date of Signature (mm/dd/yyyy)

Part 5. Signature of Attorney or Accredited Representative

I have read and understand the regulations and conditions contained in 8 CFR 103.2 and 292 governing appearances and representation before DHS. I declare under penalty of perjury under the laws of the United States that the information I have provided on this form is true and correct.

1. a. Signature of Attorney or Accredited Representative

1.b. Date of Signature (mm/dd/yyyy)

2.a. Signature of Law Student or Law Graduate

2.b. Date of Signature (mm/dd/yyyy)

Part 6. Additional Information

If you need extra space to provide any additional information within this form, use the space below. If you need more space than what is provided, you may make copies of this page to complete and file with this form or attach a separate sheet of paper. Type or print your name at the top of each sheet; indicate the **Page Number**, **Part Number**, and **Item Number** to which your answer refers; and sign and date each sheet.

1.a Family Name (Last Name) [redacted]

1.b. Given Name (First Name)

1.c. Middle Name

2.a. Page Number 2.b. Part Number 2.c. Item Number

2.d.

3.a. Page Number 3.b. Part Number 3.c. Item Number

3.d.

4.a. Page Number 4.b. Part Number 4.c. Item Number

4.d.

5.a. Page Number 5.b. Part Number 5.c. Item Number

5.d.

6.a. Page Number 6.b. Part Number 6.c. Item Number

6.d.

Notice of Entry of Appearance as Attorney or Accredited Representative

Department of Homeland Security

DHS Form G-28
OMB No. 1615-0105
Expires 05/31/2021

Part 1. Information About Attorney or Accredited Representative

1. USCIS Online Account Number (if any) ▶

Name of Attorney or Accredited Representative

2.a. Family Name (Last Name): Lerner
2.b. Given Name (First Name): Brian
2.c. Middle Name: David

Address of Attorney or Accredited Representative

3.a. Street Number and Name: 3233 E Broadway
3.b. ☐ Apt. ☐ Ste. ☐ Flr.
3.c. City or Town: Long Beach
3.d. State: CA 3.e. ZIP Code: 90803
3.f. Province:
3.g. Postal Code:
3.h. Country: USA

Contact Information of Attorney or Accredited Representative

4. Daytime Telephone Number: 5624950554
5. Mobile Telephone Number (if any):
6. Email Address (if any): blerner@californiaimmigration.us
7. Fax Number (if any): 5626088672

Part 2. Eligibility Information for Attorney or Accredited Representative

Select **all applicable** items.

1.a. ☒ I am an attorney eligible to practice law in, and a member in good standing of, the bar of the highest courts of the following states, possessions, territories, commonwealths, or the District of Columbia. If you need extra space to complete this section, use the space provided in **Part 6. Additional Information.**

Licensing Authority: Supreme Court of California

1.b. Bar Number (if applicable): 158536

1.c. I (select **only one** box) ☒ am not ☐ am subject to any order suspending, enjoining, restraining, disbarring, or otherwise restricting me in the practice of law. If you are subject to any orders, use the space provided in **Part 6. Additional Information** to provide an explanation.

1.d. Name of Law Firm or Organization (if applicable): Law Offices of Brian D. Lerner, APC

2.a. ☐ I am an accredited representative of the following qualified nonprofit religious, charitable, social service, or similar organization established in the United States and recognized by the Department of Justice in accordance with 8 CFR part 1292.

2.b. Name of Recognized Organization:

2.c. Date of Accreditation (mm/dd/yyyy):

3. ☐ I am associated with ____________, the attorney or accredited representative of record who previously filed Form G-28 in this case, and my appearance as an attorney or accredited representative for a limited purpose is at his or her request.

4.a. ☐ I am a law student or law graduate working under the direct supervision of the attorney or accredited representative of record on this form in accordance with the requirements in 8 CFR 292.1(a)(2).

4.b. Name of Law Student or Law Graduate:

Part 3. Notice of Appearance as Attorney or Accredited Representative

If you need extra space to complete this section, use the space provided in **Part 6. Additional Information**.

This appearance relates to immigration matters before (select **only one** box):

1.a. ☐ U.S. Citizenship and Immigration Services (USCIS)

1.b. List the form numbers or specific matter in which appearance is entered.

2.a. ☐ U.S. Immigration and Customs Enforcement (ICE)

2.b. List the specific matter in which appearance is entered.

3.a. ☐ U.S. Customs and Border Protection (CBP)

3.b. List the specific matter in which appearance is entered.

4. Receipt Number (if any)

▶

5. I enter my appearance as an attorney or accredited representative at the request of the (select **only one** box):

☐ Applicant ☐ Petitioner ☐ Requestor

☒ Beneficiary/Derivative ☐ Respondent (ICE, CBP)

Information About Client (Applicant, Petitioner, Requestor, Beneficiary or Derivative, Respondent, or Authorized Signatory for an Entity)

6.a. Family Name (Last Name) [redacted]

6.b. Given Name (First Name) [redacted]

6.c. Middle Name [redacted]

7.a. Name of Entity (if applicable)

7.b. Title of Authorized Signatory for Entity (if applicable)

8. Client's USCIS Online Account Number (if any)

▶

9. Client's Alien Registration Number (A-Number) (if any)

▶ **A-**

Client's Contact Information

10. Daytime Telephone Number [redacted]

11. Mobile Telephone Number (if any) [redacted]

12. Email Address (if any) [redacted]

Mailing Address of Client

NOTE: Provide the client's mailing address. **Do not** provide the business mailing address of the attorney or accredited representative **unless** it serves as the safe mailing address on the application or petition being filed with this Form G-28.

13.a. Street Number and Name [redacted]

13.b. ☐ Apt. ☒ Ste. ☐ Flr.

13.c. City or Town [redacted]

13.d. State **13.e.** ZIP Code

13.f. Province Jalisco

13.g. Postal Code [redacted]

13.h. Country

México

Part 4. Client's Consent to Representation and Signature

Consent to Representation and Release of Information

I have requested the representation of and consented to being represented by the attorney or accredited representative named in **Part 1.** of this form. According to the Privacy Act of 1974 and U.S. Department of Homeland Security (DHS) policy, I also consent to the disclosure to the named attorney or accredited representative of any records pertaining to me that appear in any system of records of USCIS, ICE, or CBP.

Part 4. Client's Consent to Representation and Signature (continued)

Options Regarding Receipt of USCIS Notices and Documents

USCIS will send notices to both a represented party (the client) and his, her, or its attorney or accredited representative either through mail or electronic delivery. USCIS will send all secure identity documents and Travel Documents to the client's U.S. mailing address.

If you want to have notices and/or secure identity documents sent to your attorney or accredited representative of record rather than to you, please select **all applicable** items below. You may change these elections through written notice to USCIS.

1.a. [X] I request that USCIS send original notices on an application or petition to the U.S. business address of my attorney or accredited representative as listed in this form.

1.b. [ ] I request that USCIS send any secure identity document (Permanent Resident Card, Employment Authorization Document, or Travel Document) that I receive to the U.S. business address of my attorney or accredited representative (or to a designated military or diplomatic address in a foreign country (if permitted)).

NOTE: If your notice contains Form I-94, Arrival-Departure Record, USCIS will send the notice to the U.S. business address of your attorney or accredited representative. If you would rather have your Form I-94 sent directly to you, select **Item Number 1.c.**

1.c. [X] I request that USCIS send my notice containing Form I-94 to me at my U.S. mailing address.

Signature of Client or Authorized Signatory for an Entity

2.a. Signature of Client or Authorized Signatory for an Entity

➡ ______________________

2.b. Date of Signature (mm/dd/yyyy) ______________

Part 5. Signature of Attorney or Accredited Representative

I have read and understand the regulations and conditions contained in 8 CFR 103.2 and 292 governing appearances and representation before DHS. I declare under penalty of perjury under the laws of the United States that the information I have provided on this form is true and correct.

1. a. Signature of Attorney or Accredited Representative

____

1.b. Date of Signature (mm/dd/yyyy) ______________

2.a. Signature of Law Student or Law Graduate

____

2.b. Date of Signature (mm/dd/yyyy) ______________

Part 6. Additional Information

If you need extra space to provide any additional information within this form, use the space below. If you need more space than what is provided, you may make copies of this page to complete and file with this form or attach a separate sheet of paper. Type or print your name at the top of each sheet; indicate the **Page Number**, **Part Number**, and **Item Number** to which your answer refers; and sign and date each sheet.

1.a Family Name (Last Name) [redacted]

1.b. Given Name (First Name) [redacted]

1.c. Middle Name [redacted]

2.a. Page Number **2.b.** Part Number **2.c.** Item Number

2.d.

BENEFICIARY'S FULL ADDRESS IN [redacted]

3.a. Page Number **3.b.** Part Number **3.c.** Item Number

3.d.

4.a. Page Number **4.b.** Part Number **4.c.** Item Number

4.d.

5.a. Page Number **5.b.** Part Number **5.c.** Item Number

5.d.

6.a. Page Number **6.b.** Part Number **6.c.** Item Number

6.d.

Petition for Alien Relative

Department of Homeland Security
U.S. Citizenship and Immigration Services

USCIS
Form I-130
OMB No. 1615-0012
Expires 07/31/2018

For USCIS Use Only		Fee Stamp	Action Stamp
A-Number A-			
Initial Receipt			
Resubmitted			
Relocated	Section of Law/Visa Category		
Received	☐ 201(b) Spouse - IR-1/CR-1 ☐ 203(a)(1) Unm. S/D - F1-1 ☐ 203(a)(2)(B) Unm. S/D - F2-4		
Sent	☐ 201(b) Child - IR-2/CR-2 ☐ 203(a)(2)(A) Spouse - F2-1 ☐ 203(a)(3) Married S/D - F3-1		
Completed	☐ 201(b) Parent - IR-5 ☐ 203(a)(2)(A) Child - F2-2 ☐ 203(a)(4) Brother/Sister - F4-1		
Approved	Petition was filed on (Priority Date mm/dd/yyyy):	☐ Field Investigation ☐ Previously Forwarded ☐ 203(g) Resolved	☐ Personal Interview ☐ Pet. A-File Reviewed ☐ Ben. A-File Reviewed ☐ 204(a)(2)(A) Resolved ☐ I-485 Filed Simultaneously ☐ 204(g) Resolved
Returned	PDR request granted/denied - New priority date (mm/dd/yyyy):		
Remarks			

At which USCIS office (e.g., NBC, VSC, LOS, CRO) was Form I-130 adjudicated? ____________

To be completed by an attorney or accredited representative (if any).			
☒ **Select this box if Form G-28 is attached.**	**Volag Number** (if any)	**Attorney State Bar Number** (if applicable)	**Attorney or Accredited Representative USCIS Online Account Number** (if any)

► **START HERE - Type or print in black ink.**

If you need extra space to complete any section of this petition, use the space provided in **Part 9. Additional Information. Complete and submit as many copies of Part 9., as necessary, with your petition.**

Part 1. Relationship (You are the Petitioner. Your relative is the Beneficiary)

1. I am filing this petition for my (Select **only one** box):
   ☒ Spouse ☐ Parent ☐ Brother/Sister ☐ Child
2. If you are filing this petition for your child or parent, select the box that describes your relationship (Select **only one** box):
   ☐ Child was born to parents who were married to each other at the time of the child's birth
   ☐ Stepchild/Stepparent
   ☐ Child was born to parents who were not married to each other at the time of the child's birth
   ☐ Child was adopted (not an Orphan or Hague Convention adoptee)
3. If the beneficiary is your brother/sister, are you related by adoption? ☐ Yes ☐ No
4. Did you gain lawful permanent resident status or citizenship through adoption? ☐ Yes ☒ No

Part 2. Information About You (Petitioner)

1. Alien Registration Number (A-Number) (if any) ► A-
2. USCIS Online Account Number (if any) ►
3. U.S. Social Security Number (if any) ►

Your Full Name

4.a. Family Name (Last Name)
4.b. Given Name (First Name)
4.c. Middle Name

Part 2. Information About You (Petitioner) (continued)

***Other Names Used** (if any)*

Provide all other names you have ever used, including aliases, maiden name, and nicknames.

5.a. Family Name (Last Name)

5.b. Given Name (First Name)

5.c. Middle Name

Other Information

6. City/Town/Village of Birth

7. Country of Birth

8. Date of Birth (mm/dd/yyyy) 10/25/1965

9. Sex ☒ Male ☐ Female

Mailing Address

10.a. In Care Of Name

10.b. Street Number and Name

10.c. ☐ Apt. ☐ Ste. ☐ Flr.

10.d. City or Town

10.e. State CA 10.f. ZIP Code

10.g. Province

10.h. Postal Code

10.i. Country USA

11. Is your current mailing address the same as your physical address? ☒ Yes ☐ No

If you answered "No" to **Item Number 11.**, provide information on your physical address in **Item Numbers 12.a. - 13.b.**

Address History

Provide your physical addresses for the last five years, whether inside or outside the United States. Provide your current address first if it is different from your mailing address in **Item Numbers 10.a. - 10.i.**

Physical Address 1

12.a. Street Number and Name

12.b. ☐ Apt. ☐ Ste. ☐ Flr.

12.c. City or Town

12.d. State 12.e. ZIP Code

12.f. Province

12.g. Postal Code

12.h. Country

13.a. Date From (mm/dd/yyyy)

13.b. Date To (mm/dd/yyyy) PRESENT

Physical Address 2

14.a. Street Number and Name

14.b. ☐ Apt. ☐ Ste. ☐ Flr.

14.c. City or Town

14.d. State CA 14.e. ZIP Code

14.f. Province

14.g. Postal Code

14.h. Country USA

15.a. Date From (mm/dd/yyyy) 03/2017

15.b. Date To (mm/dd/yyyy) 12/2017

Your Marital Information

16. How many times have you been married? ► 2

17. Current Marital Status

☐ Single, Never Married ☒ Married ☐ Divorced

☐ Widowed ☐ Separated ☐ Annulled

Part 2. Information About You (Petitioner) (continued)

18. Date of Current Marriage (if currently married) (mm/dd/yyyy) **12/16/1997**

Place of Your Current Marriage (if married)

19.a. City or Town [redacted]

19.b. State

19.c. Province [redacted]

19.d. Country **Mexico**

Names of All Your Spouses (if any)

Provide information on your current spouse (if currently married) first and then list all your prior spouses (if any).

Spouse 1

20.a. Family Name (Last Name) [redacted]

20.b. Given Name (First Name) [redacted]

20.c. Middle Name [redacted]

21. Date Marriage Ended (mm/dd/yyyy)

Spouse 2

22.a. Family Name (Last Name) [redacted]

22.b. Given Name (First Name) [redacted]

22.c. Middle Name [redacted]

23. Date Marriage Ended (mm/dd/yyyy) **05/20/1996**

Information About Your Parents

Parent 1's Information

Full Name of Parent 1

24.a. Family Name (Last Name) [redacted]

24.b. Given Name (First Name) [redacted]

24.c. Middle Name [redacted]

25. Date of Birth (mm/dd/yyyy) **06/06/1937**

26. Sex ☒ Male ☐ Female

27. Country of Birth [redacted]

28. City/Town/Village of Residence **Deceased**

29. Country of Residence **Deceased**

Parent 2's Information

Full Name of Parent 2

30.a. Family Name (Last Name) [redacted]

30.b. Given Name (First Name) [redacted]

30.c. Middle Name [redacted]

31. Date of Birth (mm/dd/yyyy) **06/26/1939**

32. Sex ☐ Male ☒ Female

33. Country of Birth [redacted]

34. City/Town/Village of Residence [redacted]

35. Country of Residence [redacted]

Additional Information About You (Petitioner)

36. I am a (Select **only one** box):

☒ U.S. Citizen ☐ Lawful Permanent Resident

If you are a U.S. citizen, complete Item Number 37.

37. My citizenship was acquired through (Select **only one** box):

☐ Birth in the United States

☒ Naturalization

☐ Parents

38. Have you obtained a Certificate of Naturalization or a Certificate of Citizenship? ☒ Yes ☐ No

If you answered "Yes" to **Item Number 38.**, complete the following:

39.a. Certificate Number [redacted]

39.b. Place of Issuance **Los Angeles, CA**

Part 2. Information About You (Petitioner) (continued)

If you are a lawful permanent resident, complete **Item Numbers 40.a. - 41.**

40.a. Class of Admission

40.b. Date of Admission (mm/dd/yyyy)

Place of Admission

40.c. City or Town

40.d State

41. Did you gain lawful permanent resident status through marriage to a U.S. citizen or lawful permanent resident?

☐ Yes ☐ No

Employment History

Provide your employment history for the last five years, whether inside or outside the United States. Provide your current employment first. If you are currently unemployed, type or print "Unemployed" in **Item Number 42.**

Employer 1

42. Name of Employer/Company

Brand Energy Solutions LLC

43.a. Street Number and Name [redacted]

43.b. ☐ Apt. ☒ Ste. ☐ Flr. A-1

43.c. City or Town [redacted]

43.d. State GA **43.e.** ZIP Code [redacted]

43.f. Province

43.g. Postal Code

43.h. Country

USA

44. Your Occupation

Scaffold Builder and Insulation Installer

45.a. Date From (mm/dd/yyyy) 04/15/2018

45.b. Date To (mm/dd/yyyy) PRESENT

Employer 2

46. Name of Employer/Company

UNEMPLOYED

47.a. Street Number and Name

47.b. ☐ Apt. ☒ Ste. ☐ Flr.

47.c. City or Town

47.d. State **47.e.** ZIP Code

47.f. Province

47.g. Postal Code

47.h. Country

48. Your Occupation

Unemployed

49.a. Date From (mm/dd/yyyy) 01/2018

49.b. Date To (mm/dd/yyyy) 04/2018

Part 3. Biographic Information

NOTE: Provide the biographic information about you, the petitioner.

1. Ethnicity (Select **only one** box)

☒ Hispanic or Latino
☐ Not Hispanic or Latino

2. Race (Select **all applicable** boxes)

☐ White
☐ Asian
☐ Black or African American
☐ American Indian or Alaska Native
☐ Native Hawaiian or Other Pacific Islander

3. Height Feet [redacted] Inches [redacted]

4. Weight Pounds 1 8 0

5. Eye Color (Select **only one** box)

☐ Black ☐ Blue ☒ Brown
☐ Gray ☐ Green ☐ Hazel
☐ Maroon ☐ Pink ☐ Unknown/Other

Part 3. Biographic Information (continued)

6. Hair Color (Select **only one** box)

☐ Bald (No hair) ☒ Black ☐ Blond
☐ Brown ☐ Gray ☐ Red
☐ Sandy ☐ White ☐ Unknown/Other

Part 4. Information About Beneficiary

1. Alien Registration Number (A-Number) (if any)
► A-

2. USCIS Online Account Number (if any)
►

3. U.S. Social Security Number (if any)
►

Beneficiary's Full Name

4.a. Family Name (Last Name) [redacted]
4.b. Given Name (First Name) [redacted]
4.c. Middle Name [redacted]

Other Names Used (if any)

Provide all other names the beneficiary has ever used, including aliases, maiden name, and nicknames.

5.a. Family Name (Last Name)
5.b. Given Name (First Name)
5.c. Middle Name

Other Information About Beneficiary

6. City/Town/Village of Birth

7. Country of Birth
México

8. Date of Birth (mm/dd/yyyy) 07/29/1980

9. Sex ☐ Male ☒ Female

10. Has anyone else ever filed a petition for the beneficiary?
☐ Yes ☒ No ☐ Unknown

NOTE: Select "Unknown" *only* if you do not know, and

Beneficiary's Physical Address

If the beneficiary lives outside the United States in a home without a street number or name, leave **Item Numbers 11.a.** and **11.b.** blank.

11.a. Street Number and Name [redacted]
11.b. ☐ Apt. ☐ Ste. ☐ Flr.
11.c. City or Town [redacted]
11.d. State 11.e. ZIP Code
11.f. Province [redacted]
11.g. Postal Code [redacted]
11.h. Country
México

Other Address and Contact Information

Provide the address in the United States where the beneficiary intends to live, if different from **Item Numbers 11.a. - 11.h.** If the address is the same, type or print "SAME" in **Item Number 12.a.**

12.a Street Number and Name [redacted]
12.b. ☐ Apt. ☐ Ste. ☐ Flr.
12.c. City or Town [redacted]
12.d. State CA 12.e. ZIP Code [redacted]

Provide the beneficiary's address outside the United States, if different from **Item Numbers 11.a. - 11.h.** If the address is the same, type or print "SAME" in **Item Number 13.a.**

13.a. Street Number and Name SAME
13.b. ☐ Apt. ☐ Ste. ☐ Flr.
13.c. City or Town
13.d. Province
13.e. Postal Code
13.f. Country

14. Daytime Telephone Number (if any)

Part 4. Information About Beneficiary (continued)

15. Mobile Telephone Number (if any)

16. Email Address (if any)

Beneficiary's Marital Information

17. How many times has the beneficiary been married? ► 1

18. Current Marital Status

☐ Single, Never Married ☒ Married ☐ Divorced

☐ Widowed ☐ Separated ☐ Annulled

19. Date of Current Marriage (if currently married) (mm/dd/yyyy) 12/16/1997

Place of Beneficiary's Current Marriage (if married)

20.a. City or Town

20.b. State

20.c. Province

20.d. Country

Names of Beneficiary's Spouses (if any)

Provide information on the beneficiary's current spouse (if currently married) first and then list all the beneficiary's prior spouses (if any).

Spouse 1

21.a. Family Name (Last Name)

21.b. Given Name (First Name)

21.c. Middle Name

22. Date Marriage Ended (mm/dd/yyyy)

Spouse 2

23.a. Family Name (Last Name)

23.b. Given Name (First Name)

24. Date Marriage Ended (mm/dd/yyyy)

Information About Beneficiary's Family

Provide information about the beneficiary's spouse and children.

Person 1

25.a. Family Name (Last Name)

25.b. Given Name (First Name)

25.c. Middle Name

26. Relationship Spouse

27. Date of Birth (mm/dd/yyyy) 10/25/1965

28. Country of Birth México

Person 2

29.a. Family Name (Last Name)

29.b. Given Name (First Name)

29.c. Middle Name

30. Relationship Child

31. Date of Birth (mm/dd/yyyy) 01/05/1999

32. Country of Birth México

Person 3

33.a. Family Name (Last Name)

33.b. Given Name (First Name)

33.c. Middle Name

34. Relationship

35. Date of Birth (mm/dd/yyyy) 04/09/2003

36. Country of Birth México

Part 4. Information About Beneficiary (continued)

Person 4

37.a. Family Name (Last Name) [redacted]

37.b. Given Name (First Name)

37.c. Middle Name

38. Relationship: Child

39. Date of Birth (mm/dd/yyyy): 02/12/2014

40. Country of Birth: México

Person 5

41.a. Family Name (Last Name)

41.b. Given Name (First Name)

41.c. Middle Name

42. Relationship

43. Date of Birth (mm/dd/yyyy)

44. Country of Birth

Beneficiary's Entry Information

45. Was the beneficiary **EVER** in the United States?

☐ Yes ☒ No

If the beneficiary is currently in the United States, complete **Items Numbers 46.a. - 46.d.**

46.a. He or she arrived as a (Class of Admission):

46.b. Form I-94 Arrival-Departure Record Number

►

46.c. Date of Arrival (mm/dd/yyyy)

46.d. Date authorized stay expired, or will expire, as shown on Form I-94 or Form I-95 (mm/dd/yyyy) or type or print "D/S" for Duration of Status

47. Passport Number

48. Travel Document Number

49. Country of Issuance for Passport or Travel Document

50. Expiration Date for Passport or Travel Document (mm/dd/yyyy)

Beneficiary's Employment Information

Provide the beneficiary's current employment information (if applicable), even if they are employed outside of the United States. If the beneficiary is currently unemployed, type or print "Unemployed" in **Item Number 51.a.**

51.a. Name of Current Employer (if applicable): NONE

51.b. Street Number and Name

51.c. ☐ Apt. ☐ Ste. ☐ Flr.

51.d. City or Town

51.e. State **51.f.** ZIP Code

51.g. Province

51.h. Postal Code

51.i. Country

52. Date Employment Began (mm/dd/yyyy)

Additional Information About Beneficiary

53. Was the beneficiary **EVER** in immigration proceedings?

☐ Yes ☒ No

54. If you answered "Yes," select the type of proceedings and provide the location and date of the proceedings.

☐ Removal ☐ Exclusion/Deportation

☐ Rescission ☐ Other Judicial Proceedings

55.a. City or Town

55.b. State

56. Date (mm/dd/yyyy)

Part 4. Information About Beneficiary (continued)

If the beneficiary's native written language does not use Roman letters, type or print his or her name and foreign address in their native written language.

57.a. Family Name (Last Name)

57.b. Given Name (First Name)

57.c. Middle Name

58.a. Street Number and Name

58.b. ☐ Apt. ☐ Ste. ☐ Flr.

58.c. City or Town

58.d. Province

58.e. Postal Code

58.f. Country

If filing for your spouse, provide the last address at which you physically lived together. If you never lived together, type or print, "Never lived together" in Item Number 59.a.

59.a. Street Number and Name [redacted]

59.b. ☐ Apt. ☐ Ste. ☐ Flr.

59.c. City or Town [redacted]

59.d. State 59.e. ZIP Code

59.f. Province Jalisco

59.g. Postal Code [redacted]

59.h. Country Mexico

60.a. Date From (mm/dd/yyyy) 01/2018

60.b. Date To (mm/dd/yyyy) 02/2018

The beneficiary is in the United States and will apply for adjustment of status to that of a lawful permanent resident at the U.S. Citizenship and Immigration Services (USCIS) office in:

61.a. City or Town

61.b. State

The beneficiary will not apply for adjustment of status in the United States, but he or she will apply for an immigrant visa abroad at the U.S. Embassy or U.S. Consulate in:

62.a. City or Town [redacted]

62.b. Province [redacted]

62.c. Country Mexico

NOTE: Choosing a U.S. Embassy or U.S. Consulate outside the country of the beneficiary's last residence does not guarantee that it will accept the beneficiary's case for processing. In these situations, the designated U.S. Embassy or U.S. Consulate has discretion over whether or not to accept the beneficiary's case.

Part 5. Other Information

1. Have you **EVER** previously filed a petition for this beneficiary or any other alien? ☐ Yes ☒ No

If you answered "Yes," provide the name, place, date of filing, and the result.

2.a. Family Name (Last Name)

2.b. Given Name (First Name)

2.c. Middle Name

3.a. City or Town

3.b. State

4. Date Filed (mm/dd/yyyy)

5. Result (for example, approved, denied, withdrawn)

If you are also submitting separate petitions for other relatives, provide the names of and your relationship to each relative.

Relative 1

6.a. Family Name (Last Name)

6.b. Given Name (First Name)

6.c. Middle Name

7. Relationship

Part 5. Other Information (continued)

Relative 2

8.a. Family Name (Last Name) [ ]

8.b. Given Name (First Name) [ ]

8.c. Middle Name [ ]

9. Relationship [ ]

WARNING: USCIS investigates the claimed relationships and verifies the validity of documents you submit. If you falsify a family relationship to obtain a visa, USCIS may seek to have you criminally prosecuted.

PENALTIES: By law, you may be imprisoned for up to 5 years or fined $250,000, or both, for entering into a marriage contract in order to evade any U.S. immigration law. In addition, you may be fined up to $10,000 and imprisoned for up to 5 years, or both, for knowingly and willfully falsifying or concealing a material fact or using any false document in submitting this petition.

Part 6. Petitioner's Statement, Contact Information, Declaration, and Signature

NOTE: Read the **Penalties** section of the Form I-130 Instructions before completing this part.

Petitioner's Statement

NOTE: Select the box for either **Item Number 1.a.** or **1.b.** If applicable, select the box for **Item Number 2.**

1.a. [X] I can read and understand English, and I have read and understand every question and instruction on this petition and my answer to every question.

1.b. [ ] The interpreter named in **Part 7.** read to me every question and instruction on this petition and my answer to every question in [ ], a language in which I am fluent. I understood all of this information as interpreted.

2. [ ] At my request, the preparer named in **Part 8.**, Brian D. Lerner, prepared this petition for me based only upon information I provided or authorized.

Petitioner's Contact Information

3. Petitioner's Daytime Telephone Number

4. Petitioner's Mobile Telephone Number (if any)

5. Petitioner's Email Address (if any)

Petitioner's Declaration and Certification

Copies of any documents I have submitted are exact photocopies of unaltered, original documents, and I understand that USCIS may require that I submit original documents to USCIS at a later date. Furthermore, I authorize the release of any information from any of my records that USCIS may need to determine my eligibility for the immigration benefit I seek.

I further authorize release of information contained in this petition, in supporting documents, and in my USCIS records to other entities and persons where necessary for the administration and enforcement of U.S. immigration laws.

I understand that USCIS may require me to appear for an appointment to take my biometrics (fingerprints, photograph, and/or signature) and, at that time, if I am required to provide biometrics, I will be required to sign an oath reaffirming that:

1) I provided or authorized all of the information contained in, and submitted with, my petition;

2) I reviewed and understood all of the information in, and submitted with, my petition; and

3) All of this information was complete, true, and correct at the time of filing.

I certify, under penalty of perjury, that all of the information in my petition and any document submitted with it were provided or authorized by me, that I reviewed and understand all of the information contained in, and submitted with, my petition, and that all of this information is complete, true, and correct.

Petitioner's Signature

6.a. Petitioner's Signature (sign in ink)

➡ [ ]

6.b. Date of Signature (mm/dd/yyyy) [ ]

NOTE TO ALL PETITIONERS: If you do not completely fill out this petition or fail to submit required documents listed in the Instructions, USCIS may deny your petition.

Part 7. Interpreter's Contact Information, Certification, and Signature

Provide the following information about the interpreter if you used one.

Interpreter's Full Name

1.a. Interpreter's Family Name (Last Name)

1.b. Interpreter's Given Name (First Name)

2. Interpreter's Business or Organization Name (if any)

Interpreter's Mailing Address

3.a. Street Number and Name

3.b. ☐ Apt. ☐ Ste. ☐ Flr.

3.c. City or Town

3.d. State **3.e.** ZIP Code

3.f. Province

3.g. Postal Code

3.h. Country

Interpreter's Contact Information

4. Interpreter's Daytime Telephone Number

5. Interpreter's Mobile Telephone Number (if any)

6. Interpreter's Email Address (if any)

Interpreter's Certification

I certify, under penalty of perjury, that:

I am fluent in English and ____________,

which is the same language provided in **Part 6., Item Number 1.b.**, and I have read to this petitioner in the identified language every question and instruction on this petition and his or her answer to every question. The petitioner informed me that he or she understands every instruction, question, and answer on the petition, including the **Petitioner's Declaration and Certification**, and has verified the accuracy of every answer.

Interpreter's Signature

7.a. Interpreter's Signature (sign in ink)

7.b. Date of Signature (mm/dd/yyyy)

Part 8. Contact Information, Declaration, and Signature of the Person Preparing this Petition, if Other Than the Petitioner

Provide the following information about the preparer.

Preparer's Full Name

1.a. Preparer's Family Name (Last Name)

Lerner

1.b. Preparer's Given Name (First Name)

Brian

2. Preparer's Business or Organization Name (if any)

Law Offices of Brian D. Lerner, APC

Preparer's Mailing Address

3.a. Street Number and Name: 3233 E. Broadway

3.b. ☐ Apt. ☐ Ste. ☐ Flr.

3.c. City or Town: Long Beach

3.d. State: CA **3.e.** ZIP Code: 90803

3.f. Province

3.g. Postal Code

3.h. Country

USA

Part 8. Contact Information, Declaration, and Signature of the Person Preparing this Petition, if Other Than the Petitioner (continued)

Preparer's Contact Information

4. Preparer's Daytime Telephone Number

5. Preparer's Mobile Telephone Number (if any)

6. Preparer's Email Address (if any)

Preparer's Statement

7.a. ☐ I am not an attorney or accredited representative but have prepared this petition on behalf of the petitioner and with the petitioner's consent.

7.b. ☒ I am an attorney or accredited representative and my representation of the petitioner in this case ☒ extends ☐ does not extend beyond the preparation of this petition.

NOTE: If you are an attorney or accredited representative whose representation extends beyond preparation of this petition, you may be obliged to submit a completed Form G-28, Notice of Entry of Appearance as Attorney or Accredited Representative, with this petition.

Preparer's Certification

By my signature, I certify, under penalty of perjury, that I prepared this petition at the request of the petitioner. The petitioner then reviewed this completed petition and informed me that he or she understands all of the information contained in, and submitted with, his or her petition, including the **Petitioner's Declaration and Certification**, and that all of this information is complete, true, and correct. I completed this petition based only on information that the petitioner provided to me or authorized me to obtain or use.

Preparer's Signature

8.a. Preparer's Signature (sign in ink)

8.b. Date of Signature (mm/dd/yyyy)

Part 9. Additional Information

If you need extra space to provide any additional information within this petition, use the space below. If you need more space than what is provided, you may make copies of this page to complete and file with this petition or attach a separate sheet of paper. Type or print your name and A-Number (if any) at the top of each sheet; indicate the **Page Number, Part Number,** and **Item Number** to which your answer refers; and sign and date each sheet.

1.a. Family Name (Last Name) [redacted]

1.b. Given Name (First Name)

1.c. Middle Name

2. A-Number (if any) ▶ **A-**

3.a. Page Number **3.b.** Part Number **3.c.** Item Number

3.d.

4.a. Page Number **4.b.** Part Number **4.c.** Item Number

4.d.

5.a. Page Number **5.b.** Part Number **5.c.** Item Number

5.d.

6.a. Page Number **6.b.** Part Number **6.c.** Item Number

6.d.

7.a. Page Number **7.b.** Part Number **7.c.** Item Number

7.d.

Addendum

, **Form: I-130 (Page 1)**

Part 2. Additional Residential History:

Part 2.: Additional Employment History of Petitioner:

Employer: ELECTRICIAN BY OWN BUSSINES
Address:
Type of Work: ELECTRICIAN
Period: 01/01/2012 - 12/01/2014

Page 2 Part 2 Items 14a-15b PETITIONER'S ADDITIONAL ADDRESS HISTORY

DATES: 01/2018-02/2018
ADDRESS:

DATES: 04/2017-12/2017
ADDRESS:

DATES: 12/20/2016-03/2017
ADDRESS:

DATES: 01/2015-11/2016
ADDRESS:

DATES: 11/2011-12/2017
ADDRESS:

Page 4 Part 2 Items 46-49b PETITIONER'S ADDITIONAL EMPLOYMENT

DATES: 04/2017-12/2017
EMPLOYER: Brand Energy Solutions, LLC

DATES 12/2016-03/2017
EMPLOYER: Unemployed

DATES 01/2015-12/2016
EMPLOYER: 3B Windows and Doors, Inc.

DATES: 01/2012-12/2014
EMPLOYER: Self Employed (Electrician)

EXHIBITS

EXHIBIT '1':
Mexican Passport of the Petitioner

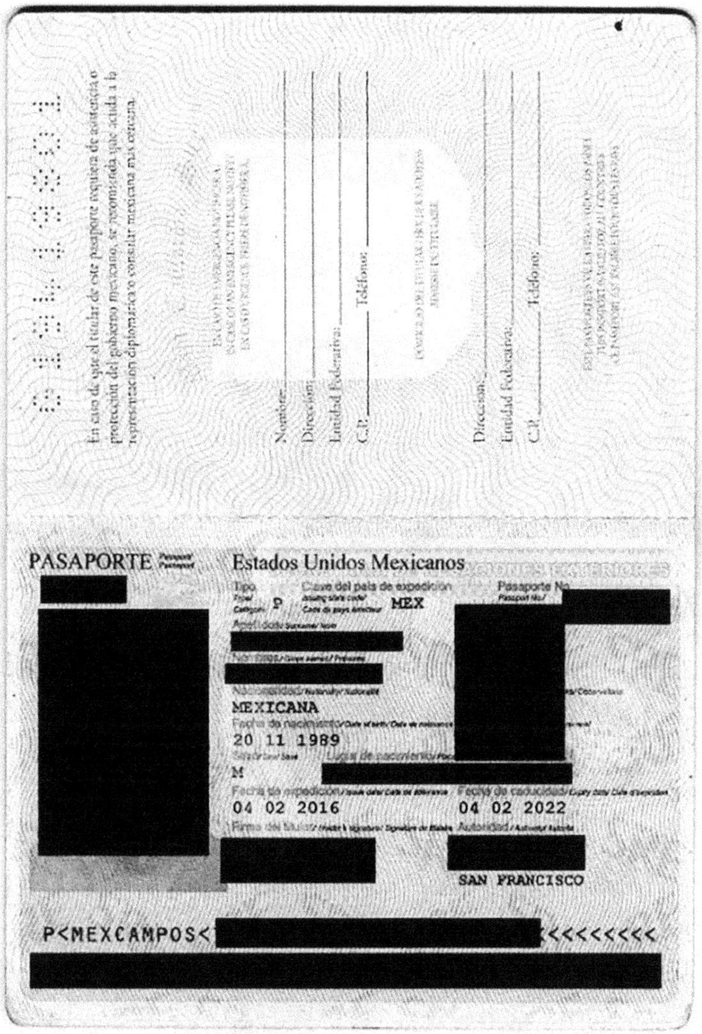
PASAPORTE
Estados Unidos Mexicanos
Tipo
P
Clave del país de expedición
MEX
Pasaporte No.
Apellidos
Nombres
Nacionalidad
MEXICANA
Fecha de nacimiento
20 11 1989
Sexo
M
Lugar de nacimiento
Fecha de expedición
04 02 2016
Fecha de caducidad
04 02 2022
Firma del titular
Autoridad
SAN FRANCISCO
P<MEXCAMPOS< <<<<<<<<

EXHIBIT '2':

Birth Certificate of the Petitioner with an English Translation

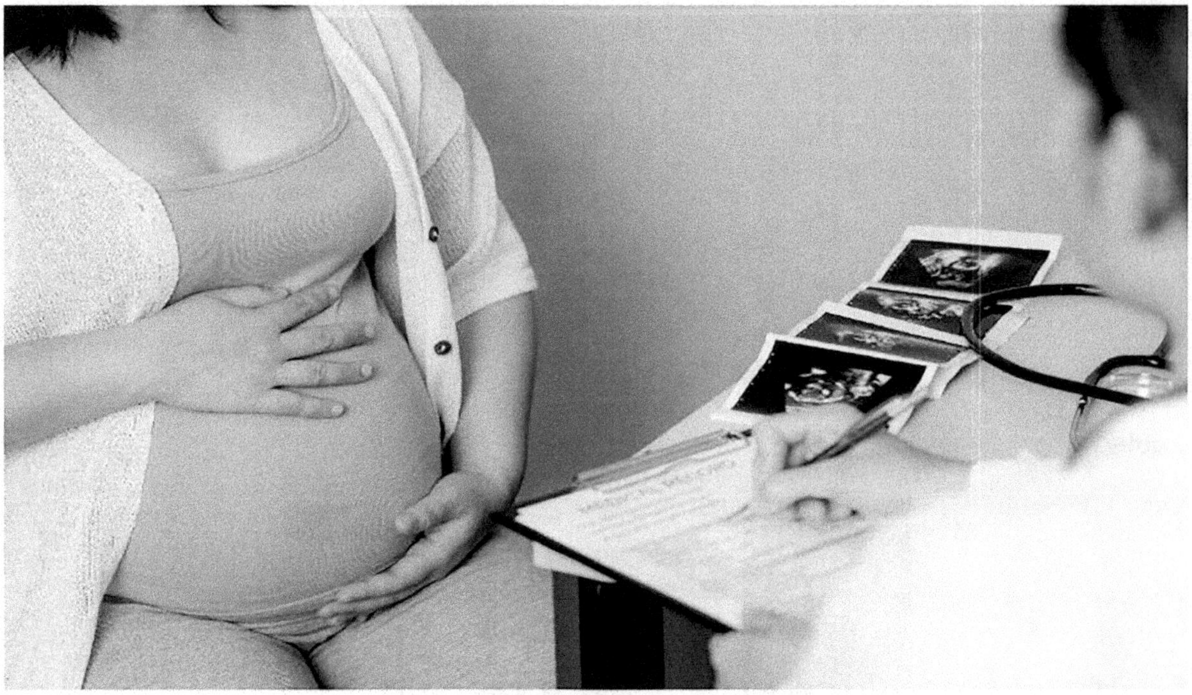

ESTADOS UNIDOS MEXICANOS

FOLIO : 39630

ESTADO LIBRE Y SOBERANO DE JALISCO

REGISTRO CIVIL DE ZAPOPAN

EL(a) C. LIC. HERLINDA LAILA ABDALA CAMPOS OFICIAL DEL REGISTRO CIVIL CON FUNDAMENTO EN EL ART. 21 FRACCION II DE LA LEY DEL REGISTRO CIVIL DEL ESTADO, CERTIFICA Y HACE CONSTAR QUE LA PRESENTE ES COPIA FIEL DEL ACTA DE

NACIMIENTO No. 1776 DEL LIBRO DUPLICADO No. 9

CORRESPONDIENTE AL AÑO 1989 DE LA OFICINA No. 2 DEL MUNICIPIO DE ZAPOPAN JALISCO

CURP CATC891120HJCMRR05

141200289017766

No. 046493

ESTADOS UNIDOS MEXICANOS

ESTADO DE JALISCO

REGISTRO CIVIL

No. DE CONTROL

ACTA DE NACIMIENTO

ACTA ORIGINAL

CLAVE ÚNICA DEL REG. DE POBLACIÓN

OFICIALÍA No.	LIBRO No.	ACTA No.	LOCALIDAD O DELEGACIÓN	FECHA DE REGISTRO DÍA	MES	AÑO
02	09	1776	PLAZA DEL SOL	20	12	89
MUNICIPIO	ZAPOPAN		ENTIDAD FEDERATIVA: JALISCO			

REGISTRADO

SEXO: MASCULINO (X) FEMENINO ( )

NOMBRE

FECHA DE NACIMIENTO ochenta y nueve

LUGAR DE NACIMIENTO

FUE REGISTRADO: VIVO (X) MUERTO ( )

No. DE CERTIFICADO DE NACIMIENTO = = = = =

COMPARECIO: EL PADRE ( ) LA MADRE (X) AMBOS ( ) PERSONA DISTINTA ( )

PADRES

NOMBRE DEL PADRE Juan Carlos Campos Torres NACIONALIDAD Mexicana EDAD 19 AÑOS

DOMICILIO Orquidea 116, Agricola, Zapopan, Jalisco

NOMBRE DE LA MADRE María Guadalupe Trujillo Monje NACIONALIDAD Mexicana EDAD 19 AÑOS

DOMICILIO en el antes citado

ABUELOS

ABUELO PATERNO Crisanto Campos Iñiguez NACIONALIDAD Mexicana

ABUELA PATERNA María Guadalupe Torres Alejo NACIONALIDAD Mexicana

DOMICILIO(S) en el mismo que los comparecientes

ABUELO MATERNO José Trujillo García NACIONALIDAD Mexicana

ABUELA MATERNA Julia Monje Lopez NACIONALIDAD Mexicana

DOMICILIO(S) en el mismo que los comparecientes

TESTIGOS

NOMBRE Susana Villaseñor Pérez NACIONALIDAD Mexicana EDAD 28 AÑOS

DOMICILIO Mariano Otero 2211, La Calma, Zapopan, Jalisco

NOMBRE Dolores Alcaraz García NACIONALIDAD Mexicana EDAD 27 AÑOS

DOMICILIO Carnero 5224, Arboledas, Zapopan, Jalisco

PERSONA DISTINTA DE LOS PADRES QUE PRESENTA AL REGISTRADO

NOMBRE = = = = = = = = = = = = = = = = = = = PARENTESCO = = = = = = = EDAD = = AÑOS

DOMICILIO =

FIRMAS DE LOS PADRES O DE LA PERSONA DISTINTA QUE PRESENTA AL REGISTRADO

maria guadalupe trujillo monje

FIRMAS DE LOS TESTIGOS

SusaVillaseñor

HUELLA DIGITAL DEL REGISTRADO

SE DIO LECTURA A LA PRESENTE ACTA Y CONFORMES CON SU CONTENIDO LA RATIFICAN Y FIRMAN QUIENES EN ELLA INTERVINIERON Y SABEN HACERLO Y QUIENES NO IMPRIMEN SU HUELLA DIGITAL. DOY FE.

EL C. OFICIAL 02 DEL REGISTRO CIVIL

C. HILDA MARTHA RAMOS RUIZ.

FIRMA

*** English Extract of Spanish Birth Certificate***
Civil Registration

Name of Registered Child:	
Sex:	Male
Date of Birth:	11/20/1989
Place of Birth:	Guadalajara, Guadalajara, Jalisco
Father of Child:	
Nationality:	Mexican
Age:	19
Mother of Child:	
Nationality:	Mexican
Age	19

Certificate Information

Issue Date:	12/20/1989
Place of Issue:	
Magistrate:	
Record Location:	Plaza Del Sol
Certificate:	
Folio:	02
Book:	09

Translator's Certificate of Competence

I, certify that the above is an accurate translation of the original Birth Certificate in Spanish and that I am competent in both English and Spanish to render such translation.

06.06.2018
Date

Law Offices of Brian D. Lerner

EXHIBIT '3':
California State Driver's License

CALIFORNIA
IDENTIFICATION CARD
EXP 06/15/2021
LN
DOB 06/15/1993
SEX F
HAIR BLK
EYES BRN
HGT 5'-01"

EXHIBIT '4':
Birth Certificate of the Beneficiary with an English Translation

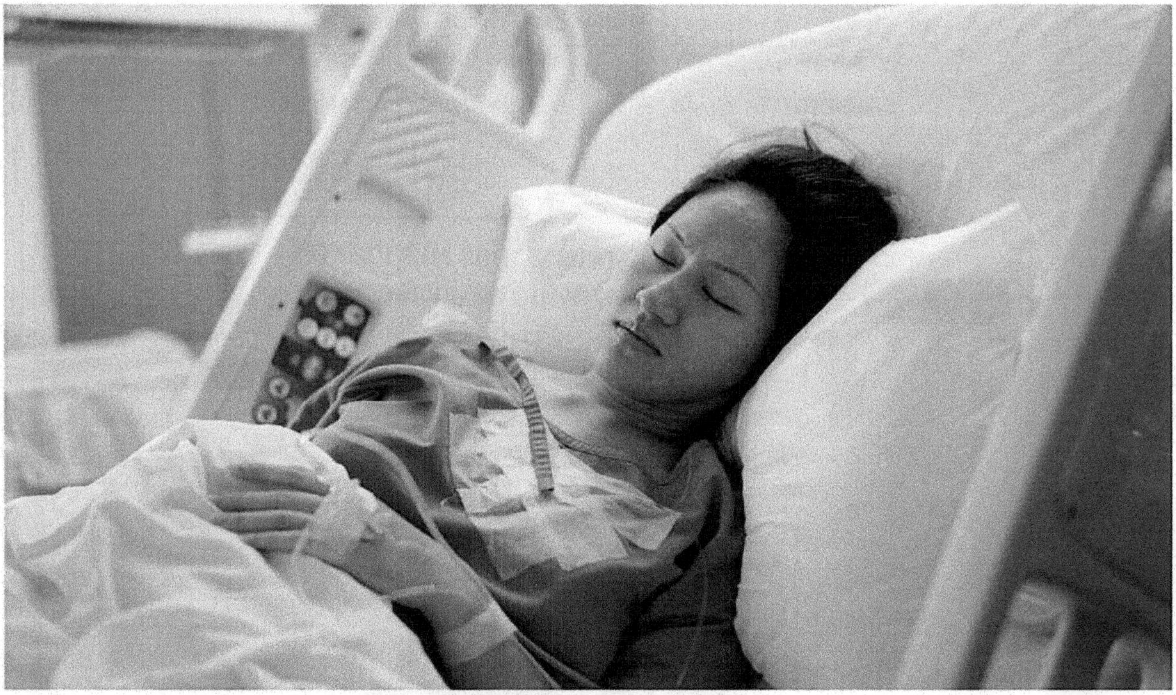

ESTADOS UNIDOS MEXICANOS

FOLIO :

ESTADO LIBRE Y SOBERANO DE JALISCO

REGISTRO CIVIL DE ZAPOPAN

EL(a) C. LIC. HERLINDA LAILA ABDALA CAMPOS OFICIAL DEL REGISTRO CIVIL CON FUNDAMENTO EN EL ART. 21 FRACCION II DE LA LEY DEL REGISTRO CIVIL DEL ESTADO, CERTIFICA Y HACE CONSTAR QUE LA PRESENTE ES COPIA FIEL DEL ACTA DE

NACIMIENTO No. 1776 DEL LIBRO DUPLICADO No. 9

CORRESPONDIENTE AL AÑO 1989 DE LA OFICINA No. 2 DEL MUNICIPIO DE ZAPOPAN JALISCO.

CURP

141200289017766

ESTADOS UNIDOS MEXICANOS

ESTADO DE JALISCO

REGISTRO CIVIL

ACTA DE NACIMIENTO

ACTA ORIGINAL

OFICIALIA No.	LIBRO No.	ACTA No.	LOCALIDAD		FECHA DE REGISTRO DIA	MES	AÑO
02	09	1776	PLAZA DEL SOL				
MUNICIPIO		ZAPOPAN	ENTIDAD FEDERATIVA	JALISCO	20	12	89

REGISTRADO

SEXO: MASCULINO (X) FEMENINO ( )

NOMBRE

FECHA DE NACIMIENTO 20, veinte de noviembre de 1989, mil novecientos ochenta y nueve HORA 8:45

LUGAR DE NACIMIENTO Guadalajara, Guadalajara, Jalisco

FUE REGISTRADO: VIVO (X) MUERTO ( ) No. DE CERTIFICADO DE NACIMIENTO = = = = =

COMPARECIO: EL PADRE ( ) LA MADRE (X) AMBOS ( ) PERSONA DISTINTA ( )

PADRES

NOMBRE DEL PADRE NACIONALIDAD Mexicana EDAD 19 AÑOS

DOMICILIO

NOMBRE DE LA MADRE NACIONALIDAD Mexicana EDAD 19 AÑOS

DOMICILIO en el antes citado

ABUELOS

ABUELO PATERNO NACIONALIDAD Mexicana

ABUELA PATERNA NACIONALIDAD Mexicana

DOMICILIO(S) en el mismo que los comparecientes

ABUELO MATERNO NACIONALIDAD Mexicana

ABUELA MATERNA NACIONALIDAD Mexicana

DOMICILIO(S) en el mismo que los comparecientes

TESTIGOS

NOMBRE NACIONALIDAD Mexicana EDAD 28 AÑOS

DOMICILIO

NOMBRE NACIONALIDAD Mexicana EDAD 27 AÑOS

DOMICILIO

PERSONA DISTINTA DE LOS PADRES QUE PRESENTA AL REGISTRADO

NOMBRE = = = = = = = = PARENTESCO = = = = = EDAD = = AÑOS

DOMICILIO =

FIRMAS DE LOS PADRES O DE LA PERSONA DISTINTA QUE PRESENTA AL REGISTRADO

FIRMAS DE LOS TESTIGOS

HUELLA DIGITAL DEL REGISTRADO

SE DIO LECTURA A LA PRESENTE ACTA Y CONFORMES CON SU CONTENIDO LA RATIFICAN Y FIRMAN QUIENES EN ELLA INTERVINIERON Y SABEN HACERLO Y QUIENES NO IMPRIMEN SU HUELLA DIGITAL. DOY FE.

EL C. OFICIAL 02 DEL REGISTRO CIVIL

FIRMA

*** English Extract of Spanish Birth Certificate***
Civil Registration

Name of Registered Child:	[redacted]
Sex:	Male
Date of Birth:	11/20/1989
Place of Birth:	Guadalajara, Guadalajara, Jalisco
Father of Child:	[redacted]
Nationality:	Mexican
Age:	19
Mother of Child:	[redacted]
Nationality:	Mexican
Age	19

Certificate Information

Issue Date:	12/20/1989
Place of Issue:	[redacted]
Magistrate:	[redacted]
Record Location:	Plaza Del Sol
Certificate:	[redacted]
Folio:	02
Book:	09

Translator's Certificate of Competence

I, [redacted] certify that the above is an accurate translation of the original Birth Certificate in Spanish and that I am competent in both English and Spanish to render such translation.

06.06.2018
Date

Law Offices of Brian D. Lerner

EXHIBIT '5':

Marriage Certificate of the Petitioner and Beneficiary's Parents

STATE OF CALIFORNIA

CERTIFICATION OF VITAL RECORD

COUNTY OF LOS ANGELES

REGISTRAR-RECORDER/COUNTY CLERK

CONFIDENTIAL

LICENSE AND CERTIFICATE OF MARRIAGE

MUST BE LEGIBLE - MAKE NO ERASURES, WHITEOUTS, OR OTHER ALTERATIONS

USE DARK INK ONLY

STATE FILE NUMBER | LOCAL REGISTRATION NUMBER

FIRST PERSON DATA

1A. FIRST NAME	
1B. MIDDLE	--
1C. CURRENT LAST	
1D. LAST NAME AT BIRTH (IF DIFFERENT THAN 1C)	--
2. DATE OF BIRTH (MM/DD/CCYY)	06/15/1993
3. STATE/COUNTRY OF BIRTH	CALIFORNIA
4. # PREV. MARRIAGES/SRDP	01
5A. LAST MARRIAGE/SRDP ENDED BY	DEATH / DISSO / ANNULMENT / TERM SRDP / NA
5B. DATE ENDED (MM/DD/CCYY)	10/09/2018
6. ADDRESS	
7. CITY	
8. STATE/COUNTRY	CA
9. ZIP CODE	91748
10A. FULL BIRTH NAME OF FATHER/PARENT	
10B. STATE OF BIRTH (IF OUTSIDE U.S. ENTER COUNTRY)	MEXICO
11A. FULL BIRTH NAME OF MOTHER/PARENT	
11B. STATE OF BIRTH (IF OUTSIDE U.S. ENTER COUNTRY)	MEXICO

SECOND PERSON DATA

12A. FIRST NAME	
12B. MIDDLE	--
12C. CURRENT LAST	
12D. LAST NAME AT BIRTH (IF DIFFERENT THAN 12C)	--
13. DATE OF BIRTH (MM/DD/CCYY)	08/17/1987
14. STATE/COUNTRY OF BIRTH	MEXICO
15. # PREV. MARRIAGES/SRDP	00
16A. LAST MARRIAGE/SRDP ENDED BY	DEATH / DISSO / ANNULMENT / TERM SRDP / NA
16B. DATE ENDED (MM/DD/CCYY)	--
17. ADDRESS	
18. CITY	
19. STATE/COUNTRY	CA
20. ZIP CODE	91748
21A. FULL BIRTH NAME OF FATHER/PARENT	
21B. STATE OF BIRTH (IF OUTSIDE U.S. ENTER COUNTRY)	GUATEMALA
22A. FULL BIRTH NAME OF MOTHER/PARENT	
22B. STATE OF BIRTH (IF OUTSIDE U.S. ENTER COUNTRY)	EL SALVADOR

AFFIDAVIT

WE, THE UNDERSIGNED, CURRENTLY LIVING TOGETHER AS SPOUSES, DECLARE UNDER PENALTY OF PERJURY UNDER THE LAWS OF THE STATE OF CALIFORNIA THAT WE ARE UNMARRIED AND THAT THE FOREGOING INFORMATION IS TRUE AND CORRECT TO THE BEST OF OUR KNOWLEDGE AND BELIEF. WE FURTHER DECLARE THAT NO LEGAL OBJECTION TO THE MARRIAGE, NOR TO THE ISSUANCE OF A LICENSE IS KNOWN TO US. WE ACKNOWLEDGE RECEIPT OF THE INFORMATION REQUIRED BY FAMILY CODE SECTION 358 AND HEREBY APPLY FOR A CONFIDENTIAL LICENSE AND CERTIFICATE OF MARRIAGE.

LICENSE TO MARRY

I, THE UNDERSIGNED, DO HEREBY CERTIFY THAT THE ABOVE NAMED PARTIES TO BE MARRIED HAVE PERSONALLY APPEARED BEFORE ME AND PROVED TO ME ON THE BASIS OF SATISFACTORY EVIDENCE TO BE THE PERSONS CLAIMED, OR THAT THE PERSON PERFORMING THE CEREMONY HAS PERSONALLY APPEARED BEFORE ME AND PRESENTED AN AFFIDAVIT SIGNED BY THE PARTIES TO BE MARRIED DECLARING THAT ONE OR BOTH OF THE PARTIES ARE PHYSICALLY UNABLE TO APPEAR AND EXPLAINING THE REASONS THEREFOR IN ACCORDANCE WITH FAMILY CODE SECTION 502. THE PARTIES HAVING FURTHER DECLARED THAT THEY MEET ALL OF THE REQUIREMENTS OF THE LAW, AND HAVING PAID THE FEES PRESCRIBED BY LAW, AUTHORIZATION AND LICENSE IS HEREBY GIVEN TO ANY PERSON DULY AUTHORIZED TO PERFORM A MARRIAGE CEREMONY WITHIN THE STATE OF CALIFORNIA TO SOLEMNIZE THE MARRIAGE OF THE ABOVE-NAMED PERSONS PURSUANT TO FAMILY CODE SECTION 500. NOTE: THE MARRIAGE CEREMONY MUST TAKE PLACE IN THE STATE OF CALIFORNIA.

25A. ISSUE DATE (MM/DD/CCYY)	10/25/2018
25B. EXPIRES AFTER (MM/DD/CCYY)	01/23/2019
25C. NAME OF COUNTY CLERK	
25D. SIGNATURE OF CLERK OR DEPUTY CLERK	BY ▶
25E. MARRIAGE LICENSE NUMBER	
25F. COUNTY OF ISSUE	LOS ANGELES
25G. RETURN COMPLETED MARRIAGE LICENSE TO (MAILING ADDRESS)	

NOTARY PUBLIC

A NOTARY PUBLIC OR OTHER OFFICER COMPLETING THIS CERTIFICATE VERIFIES ONLY THE IDENTITY OF THE INDIVIDUAL WHO SIGNED THE DOCUMENT TO WHICH THIS CERTIFICATE IS ATTACHED, AND NOT THE TRUTHFULNESS, ACCURACY, OR VALIDITY OF THAT DOCUMENT.

26A. STATE OF CALIFORNIA, COUNTY OF: LOS ANGELES

SUBSCRIBED AND SWORN TO (OR AFFIRMED) BEFORE ME ON THIS 24 DAY OF NOVEMBER, 20 18

PROVED TO ME ON THE BASIS OF SATISFACTORY EVIDENCE TO BE THE PERSON(S) WHO APPEARED BEFORE ME

26B. TYPED NAME OF NOTARY

26C. SIGNATURE OF NOTARY ▶

26D. AFFIX NOTARY SEAL: MARIA D. AVILA, NOTARY PUBLIC - CALIFORNIA, LOS ANGELES COUNTY, COMMISSION # 2100193, MY COMM. EXPIRES FEB. 15, 2019

CERTIFICATION OF PERSON SOLEMNIZING MARRIAGE

I, THE UNDERSIGNED, DECLARE UNDER PENALTY OF PERJURY UNDER THE LAWS OF THE STATE OF CALIFORNIA, THAT THE ABOVE NAMED PARTIES WERE JOINED BY ME IN MARRIAGE IN ACCORDANCE WITH THE LAWS OF THE STATE OF CALIFORNIA. NOTE: THE MARRIAGE CEREMONY MUST TAKE PLACE IN THE STATE OF CALIFORNIA.

27A. DATE OF MARRIAGE (MM/DD/CCYY)	11/24/2018
27B. CITY OF MARRIAGE	HUNTINGTON PARK
27C. COUNTY OF MARRIAGE	LOS ANGELES
28A. SIGNATURE	▶
28B. RELIGIOUS DENOMINATION (IF CLERGY)	
28C. NAME OF PERSON SOLEMNIZING MARRIAGE (TYPE OR PRINT CLEARLY)	
28D. OFFICIAL TITLE	MINISTER
28E. ADDRESS, CITY, STATE/COUNTRY, AND ZIP CODE	

NEW NAME(S) (IF ANY) (SEE REVERSE)

NEW MIDDLE AND LAST NAME OF PERSON LISTED IN 1A-1D (IF ANY) FOR USE UPON SOLEMNIZATION OF THE MARRIAGE (SEE REVERSE FOR INFORMATION)

29A. FIRST - MUST BE SAME AS 1A	29B. MIDDLE	29C. LAST
	--	

NEW MIDDLE AND LAST NAME OF PERSON LISTED IN 12A-12D (IF ANY) FOR USE UPON SOLEMNIZATION OF THE MARRIAGE

30A. FIRST - MUST BE SAME AS 12A	30B. MIDDLE	30C. LAST
--	--	--

COUNTY CLERK

31A. NAME OF COUNTY CLERK	31B. SIGNATURE	31C. DATE ACCEPTED FOR REGISTRATION
DEAN C. LOGAN	BY ▶	12/18/2018

CALIFORNIA DEPARTMENT OF PUBLIC HEALTH - VITAL RECORDS

VS 123 (01/01/2015)

This is to certify that this document is a true copy of the official record filed with the Registrar-Recorder/County Clerk.

Dean C. Logan

DEAN C. LOGAN

Registrar-Recorder/County Clerk

JAN 04 2019

CALOSANG02

ABOUT THE AUTHOR

Brian D. Lerner is an Immigration Lawyer and runs a National Immigration Law Firm for nearly 30 years. He is an attorney who is a certified specialist that might help in Immigration & Nationality Law as issued by the California State Bar, Board of Legal Specialization. Attorney Lerner is an expert in Immigration Law, Removal and Deportation, Citizenship, Waiver and Appeals.

He has been a licensed attorney since 1992 and started the Law Offices of Brian D. Lerner, APC. The immigration practice consists of Immigration and Nationality Law, and everything involved with and regarding immigration which includes citizenship, investment visas, family and employment visas, removal and deportation hearings, appeals, waivers, adjustment, consulate processing and all types of immigration and citizenship matters.

He has represented clients from all over the U.S. and in many countries around the world. One side of his practice is dedicated to keeping people in the U.S. and fighting for their immigration rights, while another side is to get people back who have been deported and removed from the U.S.

Also, there is the affirmative part of Immigration Law which Brian Lerner has helped numerous people come into the U.S. on business visas, investment visas, student visas, fiancée and marriage visas, religious visas and many more. Attorney Lerner has helped immigrants who are victims of crime and domestic violence or ones that are married to abusers.

In other words, Attorney Lerner has a firm that helps people all over the U.S. He has dedicated significant time to preparing numerous petitions and applications for you to get at a fraction of the price of hiring an attorney. He says it is the next best thing to a real attorney because they are real petitions prepared by an expert.

www.ingramcontent.com/pod-product-compliance
Lightning Source LLC
Chambersburg PA
CBHW061357240926
51846CB00007B/1432
* 9 7 8 1 9 5 8 9 9 0 4 0 7 *